REiKi
Touch

The Essential Handbook

REIKI Master Judy-Carol Stewart

PUBLISHED BY
The Reiki Touch, Inc.
P.O. Box 270957
Houston, Texas 77277-0957

Second Edition
First Printing - 1995

ISBN 0-9621291-1-9
Library of congress Catalog Card Number: 94-90576
Printed in the United States of America

For information on seminars, write:
The Reiki Touch, Inc.
P.O. Box 270957
Houston, Texas 77277-0957
Fax: (713) 668-5572

For additional books, call or write:
New Leaf Distributing Company
5425 Tulane Drive SW
Atlanta, Georgia USA 30336-2323
(404) 691-6996

Dedication

This book is dedicated to Creation and to all those on this Sacred Planet Earth who Touch.

Contents

About the Author

Reiki Master Judy-Carol Stewart is Founder and President of the Reiki Touch and a member of the Reiki Alliance. Judy-Carol Stewart is Reiki. She exemplifies this by traveling wherever she is invited to teach and practice Reiki. She has taught Reiki in many states in the United States, and also in England, Europe, the Orient, India, and Caribbean Islands. Judy-Carol trains individuals as Reiki Masters so that they too may perpetuate this Universal Life Force throughout the world.

May the *'Touch'* be yours!

Acknowledgements

With abundant gratitude to my Guru, by whose Grace I was born, this book was written and the truth of Reiki can be told; in London, to Barney Wan, who with his honor, tenderness and superb expertise designed the book including cover, illustrations and supervised the entire production; in San Francisco, to Bradley Bernstein, who assisted Barney with computer processing; in Hong Kong, to Margaret Tancock, who introduced me to Barney, suggesting the book "needed a little polish"; in Houston, to Mandy Stewart, my daughter, who did the original graphic design for the Protection Method; in Boston, to Sharon Seivert for her patience in editing the book; in Houston, to Cynthia Pinsonnault for her speedy and expert typesetting, also in Houston, to Morgan Bomar for fighting the final fire in the multitudinous details of final production; and last, but nowhere near least, my heartfelt gratitude to all my Reiki students and Reiki Masters all over the world – you are what makes it work. I am Grateful.

Keep climbing up the
spiritual ladder of life.
Hold out your hand
to those who desire to go up
with you as you continue to climb.

Introduction

Reiki is a time honored, sacred method of bringing balance and harmony to the body – physically, the mind – mentally, and the soul – spiritually. The ancient Tibetan Buddhist Sutras, or records, date back almost three thousand years.

Reiki has been in the oral tradition during its history so there is little to read about Reiki. It is the meditation of this author that it is time for some of the teachings to be in print for those who desire it.

The author asks the blessings and guidance of the ascended Tibetan Buddhist masters, Dr. Mikao Usui, Dr. Chujiro Hayashi, and Hawayo Takata in the manifestation of this material.

REIKI Master Judy-Carol Stewart

Dr. Mikao Usui

Dr. Chujiro Hayashi

Hawayo Takata

Grand Master Hawayo Takata's Master Certificate

This is to certify that Mrs. Hawayo Takata, an American citizen born in the territory of Hawaii, after a course of study and training in the Usui System of Reiki Healing undertaken under my personal supervision during a visit to Japan in 1935 and subsequently, has passed all the tests and proved worthy and capable of administrating the treatment and of conferring the power of Reiki on others.

Therefore, I, Dr. Chujiro Hayashi, by virtue of my authority as a Master of the Usui Reiki System of drugless healing, do hereby confer upon Mrs. Hawayo Takata the full power and authority to practice the Reiki system and to impart others the secret knowledge and the gift of healing under this system.

Mrs. Hawayo Takata is hereby certified by me as a practitioner and Master of Dr. Usui's Reiki System of Healing, at this time the only person, in the United States authorized to confer similar powers on others and one of the thirteen fully qualified as a Master of the profession.

Signed by me this 21st day of February, 1938, in the City and County of Honolulu, Territory of Hawaii.

Chujiro Hayashi

I

Origins of REIKI

On May 7, 1978, Reiki Grand Master Hawayo Takata sat at the dining room table in the Chicago home of my Reiki Master, Barbara Lincoln McCullough, and told her this story of the origins of Reiki. With great humility I present this to you.

This is the story of Dr. Usui as told to me by my teacher, Master Hayashi. I'm very sorry that I never met Dr. Usui in person. Dr. Hayashi said he was a genius! Dr. Usui was very positive and intelligent. In every aspect of his life he was above average, a perfectionist. For example, after he left Japan, he earned his living by mastering the French art of ironing dinner shirts (with starched fronts and collars).

So, even when he was a stranger in a foreign country, he earned a five dollar gold piece to finish each dress shirt. He was terrific!

Dr. Usui's real profession was as a scholar, Christian minister, teacher, and principal of the DoShiSha University in Kyoto. On Sundays he went to the chapel to deliver sermons. He was a very admired and adored teacher and minister. One Sunday he saw that about six students, who were supposed to sit in the back pew, had sat in the very front. When he started to read passages from the Bible, their hands went up. Dr Usui said, "Yes, what is it?"

One of the students replied, "Dr. Usui, we are here this morning because in a few months we will graduate. We are not little children anymore. We are adults. What we would like to know is: Do you have absolute faith in the Bible?"

Dr. Usui was surprised, but he said, "Yes. I am a minister, a teacher, and a student of the Bible. This is my word. My answer is Yes. I accept the Bible. I believe. I have faith in Christianity."

The students said, "Dr. Usui, we would like to have faith and accept Christianity as you do. But on one condition: We would like a demonstration." Dr. Usui asked them what kind of demonstration they needed. They said, "We believe that Christ walked on the water, Christ was able to heal the blind and the lame, and all these things that are in the Bible. We would like to say that everything we have learned in this school is true, but a demonstration will be necessary to prove it to us. So, if you can show us that you can walk on the water, or heal the blind or the lame, we will be willing to accept it."

To that Dr. Usui said, "I am sorry. I have not learned to do the healing, but I believe Christ did it."

The students responded, "You are the teacher. We expect you to be able to demonstrate so that we have more faith. Seeing is believing."

So Dr Usui said, "As much as I have studied and read the Bible, I am not able to do these things. However, let us not say this is the end. I will put this on top of a shelf and leave it open. Someday, when I go to a Christian country, I may find the answer. When I do, I shall come back here and demonstrate to you." And that very day Dr. Usui resigned his positions and walked out of the church.

12

Dr. Usui applied to go to America. After the visas and passport were prepared, he came to the United States and entered the University of Chicago. Isn't that strange? I am here in Chicago, telling you this story that happened here many, many years ago. Dr. Usui did research work in the subject of Christianity, but he found that the Christianity he had studied in Japan and here was the same. The Bible he held in his hand in Japan and the Bible he used here were identical. Therefore, he did not discover how Christ healed. He didn't lose faith, but he was disappointed. In Japan, Shintoism was the primary religion, then Buddhism, and then Christianity. He had thought his studies would be advanced in a Christian country, but he was disappointed.

He began to look into the different

philosophies of the world. When he studied Buddhism, he found a passage in the Buddhist Sutras which said that Buddha healed the blind, the crippled, those with tuberculosis and even leprosy. He pondered this and said to himself, "Ah, this is wonderful. Others have done the healing. For me to study Buddhism in this country is not right. I should go back to Japan, go to the old monasteries or to the Buddhism centers, and find out from the monks or the priests whether they can prove that Buddha healed." After seven years of studying philosophy in the United States, Dr. Usui went back to Japan.

Because Kyoto is a seat of religion, it has many temples, shrines and churches. The first one to which Dr. Usui ventured was the oldest Buddhist temple. He knocked at the door and said he would like to see the head monk. He was allowed in and asked what he wanted. He said, "I am a student of Buddhism, and I want to know if what is said in the Sutras about Buddha's healing is correct." The monk replied that it was. So, Dr. Usui said, "Since you are a very high monk, can you do healing? If you can, I would like to study under you. I would like to see a demonstration of the healing art."

The monk answered, "In this temple we do not do healing of the physical body. We think that the mind is more important. The work of all these priests and myself is to train the young monks and priests who are to carry on our spiritual work. For aches and pains, we have doctors who have medicines, herbs, and techniques to heal the body. The body is secondary. The mind comes first. We are trying to teach how human beings can be better, happier, more honest, kinder, more loving – people who would aid humanity. We have to prepare them from within, so they are better qualified. We are too busy with the churches, ministering, and the teachings of Buddha. We do not have time to tend to the physical needs of people."

So Dr. Usui said, "Thank you, I'll move on." He went to another temple, and then another temple. At all the temples, all the monks and priests gave the same answer: That soul saving was more important, that the stem of the physical self comes from the mind. Each time, Dr. Usui would thank them and move on.

In this way, he covered all of Kyoto. Finally he came to the last temple, a Zen monastery. He knocked at the door, and a page came out. Dr. Usui asked to see the head monk, and the page invited him in. The head monk was about seventy-two years old. He had a lovely face with very beautiful eyes. He was kindly-looking and very enlightened. He graciously welcomed Dr. Usui, and asked what he could do for him. Dr. Usui said, "I am searching. I would like to learn from the Buddhist Sutras whether Buddha really healed illnesses of the body as well as of the mind."

The monk said, "Yes, that is true." When Dr. Usui asked the monk if he had mastered the art of healing, the monk replied that he had not. "Our church is very busy, giving sermons, preaching, giving lessons, teaching common men how to better themselves and earn an honest living. All this takes time and training.

Yet we also believe in the importance of the physical because Buddha has said that all life is one, and that the body should be part of a complete whole. Therefore, our work is incomplete. True meditation in the Zen system requires hours and hours of purification of our soul and body. But someday we will be enlightened. We will be granted and surrounded by this great force – the light. Then we will be able to heal the physical body. With Zen, we do not say this is the end. We have patience. We are still learning. We are trying to gain not only knowledge, but wisdom – and it shall come to us. We have hope." When Dr. Usui heard this, he asked to be accepted as a student so that he could learn all about Buddhism, meditate with these monks, and become enlightened.

Dr. Usui took about three years to go

through all the studies. Since he was highly educated, he had no trouble reading the Sutras, which he quickly understood. He meditated with the other monks and priests. He said, "This is not enough." Since Buddhism came from China to Korea, then into Japan, he decided to study the original Chinese characters. He thought that if he mastered the Chinese characters, he might be able to interpret the Sutras better and find the formula. When he did master the Chinese characters, again he said, "This is not enough."

Since Buddha was born in India, received his enlightenment, and became the Buddha in India, Dr. Usui decided that he should study Sanskrit. It was here, among the Sanskrit writings of Buddha, that Dr. Usui finally found the formula for how to heal – how to contact the great Universal Life Force! When he found this, the rest was very simple for him because Dr. Usui was searching for it with his heart and soul.

Dr. Usui thought, "I find this to be just as clear as daylight. This is not hard, not complicated, but very ancient. I should really test it to see if this works." He talked it over with the head monk and said, "I think I should go up to Mount Kura Yama and meditate for twenty-one days. After the meditation I will come back here." He started out early the next morning. He had no timepiece. He took only water. When he went up into the mountains, he found a spot. He said, "This is where I am going to sit." Before he sat he picked up twenty-one small stones and laid them in front of him. Each day at sunrise he picked up a stone and threw it away, saying, "Ah, this is a new day and now I shall continue my meditation." He meditated; he sat and he sat.

Finally the twenty-first day arrived. When he picked up his stone he said, "This is the last day of my meditation. After this I shall walk seventeen miles to Kyoto to the temple. I will be very happy and grateful if I can go back to the temple all in one piece."

With that thought in mind, he started his meditation. It was early in the morning. Before dawn, before sunrise, is the darkest of morning. For a time he could not see the stars, not even dark clouds. Everything was so dark he could not see his hands put away from his face. But as he sat in meditation, with his eyes closed, he saw a light the size of a candle-light.

He thought it was only his imagination. Then he opened his eyes and still saw the light. When he stared at the light, it began to move towards him. He thought, "Now it is beginning to move faster and faster. It might strike me! If it strikes me, it might destroy me. It might burn my forehead." Then he thought, "Why should I run away now? I expected something, and now that it has happened, why should I run away? I will not lose any contact. I'm not even going to blink my eyes. I will brace myself and receive this strike." Soon the light hit him right in the center of his forehead. It knocked him down backwards. He did not feel any pain nor burning, but he thought he had died. He didn't remember what happened after that for awhile; everything was absolutely blank.

When he came to his senses, he slowly opened his eyes. He saw bubbles, bubbles, bubbles, a million bubbles floating from the right to the left. These bubbles had colors – fuchsia, purple, green, yellow – all the colors of the rainbow came one by one. They floated from the right to the left and passed. Dr. Usui was staring, not even batting an eye. Finally came a white light that was very powerful and bright. As he looked and looked, he saw the golden letters he had studied in the Sanskrit and in the Sutras – the secret formula of the Universal Life Force and how to contact it! The golden letters came in front of him, one by one, as if to say, "Remember this. Remember, this is the truth." He just stared and stared and tried to remember. And he remembered.

All this phenomena passed. When it ended, he found himself vitalized. He felt no thirst nor hunger. He stood up and stomped his feet, saying, "My legs have strength; they are not weak." He brushed off all the leaves, the pine needles and the dust from his gown. He shook himself and thought, "Ah, I feel very, very vitalized and very light – as if I could float. This is the first miracle. I am so happy that I am all in one piece. I know I can walk back seventeen miles to the temple. I must hurry." It was now daylight and the sun was very high. He thought, "I could almost run down the mountain" – which he did.

When he came to the foot of the hill, he stumbled against a little rock. He hurt the big toe of his left foot. He saw that the nail was turned upward, the blood streaming out from both sides. He said, "Ah, I have hurt myself," and he grabbed the toe with one hand. As soon as he grabbed the toe, he felt that something was moving, vibrating, or pulsating. He said, "Ah, the pain is going away, and I feel as if the blood has stopped flowing." He covered the foot with both hands and held it. He then felt this vibration or pulsation in both hands. He held the toe until the pulsation stopped. He took off his hands and saw that his toenail had come back to its normal position. There was no ache or pain. It had healed completely. All the blood that had run to the side was dried up. He stomped his feet again on the ground and said, "Ah, there's no pain. This is the second miracle!"

He went a few yards and found a bench

with a red blanket. In Japan, whenever you find a little isolated corner in the mountains, streets, temples or shrines which has a bench with a red blanket and a little smoking place, that means: "Any passerby, you are welcome, please sit down. There is food around the corner. Please rest and enjoy your pipe."

There was a red blanket on this bench, so Dr. Usui sat down and looked around. To the right he saw an old man just starting his charcoal stove with a fan, trying to raise the fire. On top of this charcoal stove was a kettle in which he was trying to make hot tea. The old man walked over and said, "Good morning, my dear monk. What can I do for you?" Dr. Usui said he would like to have rice, tea, and vegetables for breakfast because he had to walk all the way back to Kyoto. The old man said, "My dear monk, according to your dirty face and the growth of your beard, you have been up the mountain for twenty-one days for meditation. I know you have fasted. I cannot let you have solid food all of a sudden. You will have acute indigestion, you will double up with pain. Will you wait until this water is hot? I will make rice gruel, like mush. Then I will serve that with salted plums, salted cabbage and seaweed. You will have a nice breakfast, but please be patient." But Dr. Usui did not listen to him: He went to the platform, got the bamboo container of rice and brought it to the red blanket. He then sat and waited.

The 16-year old granddaughter came out with a rice bowl, chopsticks, tea cup and a pot of tea, plus all the breakfast food that goes with it. She said, "Good morning, my dear monk."

Dr. Usui looked into her face and asked why she was crying. She had a large towel which wrapped around her jaw and tied into rabbit ears on the top of her head. She answered, "My dear monk, I have an awful toothache. For three days and three nights I cannot stop the pain nor my tears. I have suffered and suffered, but it is too far to walk seventeen miles to Kyoto to go to the dentist, and I cannot afford a car."

Dr Usui stood up, put his right hand on her jaw, and started to feel around. When he did, he said, "Is this the tooth that is hurting you?" She nodded. He said, "Yes, that is the one! I shall hold it for a few minutes." He put both his hands on her cheeks.

In a few minutes her eyes went blink, blink, and she exclaimed, "Oh, my dear monk, this is magic! The pain is going away and I feel so much better. Now my tears have stopped." Dr. Usui held her face for a few more minutes until the pain was completely gone. She was so happy that she ran to her grandfather and said, "Grandfather, this monk is not an ordinary monk. He does magic! Through magic he treated my toothache. It's all gone now."

The grandfather was so happy. He walked toward Dr. Usui, wiping his hands on his apron, bowing very low, while saying, "My dear monk, I want to thank you for stopping that toothache. My grandchild said you just made magic and the toothache is all gone – no more tears." There was great rejoicing. The grandfather said, "You have relieved both of us, because I was suffering to see her suffer. Now she has no pain and can also eat. You have made both of us very grateful, very thankful. We offer this breakfast as gratitude. Please accept this small thing."

Dr. Usui stood up, put his hands together and said, "Thank you. I accept your gratitude. I am very fortunate that this stand was here. I could fill up my stomach, and now I can go back to Kyoto because I have the strength to walk the seventeen miles." He then opened his wallet and put thirty-five cents on the tray for the breakfast saying, "I accept your gratitude, but you need this more than I do. You are away from the city, and I may be your only guest for today. Now I have to rush to reach the temple before sundown. Good-bye and thank you."

During his walk home he was counting the miracles. First, he was not thirsty or hungry and his whole body felt vitalized. His legs were light and he could run down the hill. The second miracle was that he had stubbed his toe on a stone, but it was healed within minutes. The third was that eating the solid food after twenty-one days did not give him acute indigestion. The fourth was healing the granddaughter's toothache. When he arrived at the temple at sunset, he was not at all fatigued: It was as if he had just awakened in the morning, full of vitality. Five miracles that day!

As he arrived at the gate, the page boy came out and said, "Ah, Dr. Usui, we are very glad to see you. Welcome home. If you had not come home by the morning of the twenty-second day, we would have sent out a search party to pick up your bones. But, you are safe and sound." He continued, "Please come in and take off your slippers." When Dr. Usui sat down and asked about the head monk, the page boy said, "The monk is not feeling well. He is in bed with comforters, nursing his arthritis and the pain in his back. If you will take a bath, we will warm up your food. After dinner you can pay your respects to the monk. I am sure he is waiting for you."

Dr. Usui went for his hot bath, had his dinner, changed his clothes, and went to pay his respects to the monk. After the salutation the monk asked him how his meditation had been. "Success, success, and success," responded Dr. Usui. "I have accomplished what I was searching for." All this time Dr. Usui had both his hands on the monk's neck and shoulders, down the spine, to the hips where the pain was. During their conversation, the monk was completely healed. He was delighted! He suggested that they both rest and continue their conversation in the morning. They said goodnight and parted.

The next morning Dr. Usui woke up very fresh from a good night's sleep. He was ready for breakfast when the monk came to sit with him. He said, "Thank you, Dr. Usui, I slept well. All my aches and pains have disappeared, and my legs seem to function better." They then discussed how they could best use "Reiki" (Universal Life Force) for the advantage of mankind. After much discussion they decided that Dr. Usui would enter the large slum in Kyoto. There he could find any sort of illness: tuberculosis, leprosy, blindness, injuries, and acute pneumonia. They decided that was the place for Dr. Usui to start, to get experience healing with Reiki.

Dr. Usui disguised himself as a vegetable peddler. He took two baskets of fresh vegetables and carried them on a long pole. He went to the beggar's compound and said, "Good morning." The people were very curious: Here was a neatly clothed vegetable peddler. The first thing Dr. Usui said was, "I am one of you, and I would like to stay right here." They replied that he would have to see the Beggar Chief, whom they fetched.

The Beggar Chief looked over Dr. Usui from head to toe. He said, "If you truly wish to settle here, you have to go through initiation. The people here are very, very poor. They are professional beggars, therefore, nobody dresses like you do. Hand the vegetables over; we will relieve you of them. Tell me, what are you going to do here? You don't look like a beggar."

Dr. Usui said, "No, and I will not beg for my daily bread. You are going to feed me. But I have a wonderful profession. I am a healer. I will try to wipe out all the illness in this camp. As soon as I get settled, I will start my work. I will work from sunup until sundown. I need a room by myself so people can come over and take this treatment."

The Chief said, "Very good. We need a man like you. You can do lots for us, and we are fortunate that you have come. You shall work from sunup until sundown. You shall have a place and we will bring you food three times a day."

"Now we will have the initiation." He

turned around and told one of his men, "Bring the initiation clothes." They were brought: Rags and rags. "No one in this place has new clothes; we will relieve you of all your clothes." They took off the top clothes, the skirt, and his underwear – where they found his money belt. "Ah, just as I suspected," said the Beggar Chief. "In this camp you do not need money. There is no shopping center. We are going to feed you three meals a day." The Chief took the money belt away and left Dr. Usui to put on the old, old rags, which he tied with a sash. "Now you are one of us. You have gone through the initiation. We will show you the way to your room." They gave him a room with complete privacy so he could take in patients.

Dr. Usui started with the young ones, in their twenties, because he felt their cause was not so deep. In a few days they reported that they were beginning to change: Their aches and pains were gone, and they were sleeping better. Dr. Usui, said, "Yes, you are young and your sickness is not chronic. When you are well, I will send you to a Zen temple in a certain district. Go there, and they will give you a new name and a job. This is the first time you will live like an honorable citizen. You will be responsible for yourself." They were happy, and they went. Then he took the next person, and the next, trying to get all the young people out of this compound. Then he started on the chronic cases, the elderly, the crippled people, then the children and the babies.

Dr. Usui acted according to what he had read in the Sutras: Remove the cause and there shall be no effects. Dr. Usui was very successful in healing the physical illnesses. He was in the beggar camp for seven years. That is a long time, but he needed to practice. In the beggar kingdom he found tuberculosis, infantigo, leprosy, emphysema, and all the diseases he wanted to know about and practice on.

After seven years, he began to have a little time. At twilight he would walk around the compound wondering, "How big is this compound? How many more people?" As he was walking he found familiar faces. He stopped in front of one person, pointed his finger and said, "I know you. Somewhere I have met you, but I do not know your name."

This man smiled and said, "Of course, you know me. I am one of the first guys you helped. You sent me to the Zen temple, and I got a new name and a job. I worked as an honorable citizen, had a responsible job and was responsible for myself."

While Dr. Usui was talking, he saw another face that was familiar, and another one, and another. He asked what they were doing back in the beggar camp. They all stepped forward and said, "For the same reason. I had this certain disease, and I was healed. After I was healed, I went to the temple and got a job. But all I could stay was two years. I decided that to be an honorable citizen was very, very hard. So I came back to the beggar compound where it is easier and without responsibilities." This is the way these people responded. Dr. Usui asked each of them if it was true. They all said, "I would rather be a beggar. It is less responsibility and there is less work. To be out there in competition with the public is a great, great worry. It is better to be a beggar."

When Dr. Usui heard that from all the young people, he prostrated himself in the mud on the ground. He cried like a child, as if his heart was broken. "Oh, this is terrible! What a terrible thing I did! All the temples, all the monasteries, all the monks and priests were absolutely correct. Here I was thinking only of the physical healing. I forgot to teach them the spiritual."

"From this time on," he said, "I shall refuse all beggars. Where the fault lies is that they did not have any sense of appreciation nor gratitude. This is what the churches were trying to teach: spirituality; honest daily work; honor; gratitude toward their food, parents, teachers and neighbors. These people have failed because they have no sense of gratitude."

While Dr. Usui had his face in the ground, the five principles of Reiki were born. When he finally stood up, he wiped his tears and walked out of that beggars camp back to the temple. There he told the head monk, "I am a failure. The churches were right. I have learned."

The monk asked, "What have you learned?"
Dr. Usui replied, "Wisdom."
"And what is the wisdom?" asked the monk.
Dr. Usui responded, "I have ideals, and they are five:

"One – Just for today thou shall not anger.

"Two – Just for today thou shall not worry.

"Three –We should count our blessings and show our gratitude.

"Four – Do an honest day's job, earn
an honest living.

"Five – Be kind to anything that has
life."

It is important to show our gratitude
towards our parents, teachers and neighbors.
We should also show gratitude toward food,
because even one grain of rice that we use to
fill up our bellies did not come to our table
without a sacrifice by somebody. We should
thank God that God produced these things.
The farmer says, "I planted the seed; I culti-
vated." Yes, he did; he used his knowledge to
prepare the ground and plant the seed. But,
out of the ground the seed matures and opens
– then the little stalk comes out, perhaps two

leaves in the beginning. That is God-power, that is God, that is Reiki.

Beggars will never realize the ideals of Reiki. If we throw away even a leaf of lettuce, we are not respecting the life of the lettuce. The same thing with turnips and carrots – when we pull the carrots out of the ground and cut the tops, we kill them. They all have life. We cut and chop food to nourish our bodies. We should show our gratitude to God and never waste this God-given food. For the rice to come from the ground to our tables is no accident; it is all provided by God-power. We have famine when we waste food and do not show our gratitude.

When we were born, God gave us a very large platter of food. We should turn ourselves into little mice and very slowly, without dropping anything, nibble our food – nibble, nibble, nibble, all around the tray – so the food lasts a long time, and we have a long life.

But there are people who say, "Never mind the vegetables. I'm going to eat four kinds of meat: Fish, ham, chicken, beef, all these varieties." When they come to their middle age, they go to the doctor and the doctor tells them that because they overate meat, they can no longer eat meat or salt. They then look at their platter, and those foods are gone. Now they have to eat the leftovers.

Some people love sugar, pastries, and cookies. They go to the doctor and learn that they have diabetes. Then they look on their platter and find that all the sweets are gone – so they have to eat the leftovers. This is the way the law of truth reigns. We have to show appreciation and not waste anything. We must nibble and nibble and stretch our food so that we have a long life-line, without illness.

From that time forward, Dr. Usui refused all beggars. When we become practitioners, we see that there are many, many people who hear about Reiki. However, they will not have a chance to acquire it – when they are close, they run away. They have to go through many changes and stages of life before they will come to be helped by Reiki. Sometimes, by mere conversation, a person will accept Reiki immediately: This person is of noble character. Such people are searching. They have done their part, they have shown gratitude, and their desire is to help mankind. They are spiriitually very high and can receive Reiki as a wonderful gift.

When he returned to the temple, Dr. Usui went out with a torch into the city. A young man tapped him on the shoulder and said, "My dear monk, this is broad daylight and the sun is high. You do not need this torch."

People gathered. Dr. Usui said, "I am searching for people with hearts full of love, people who have enlightened hearts but who also need help. If you wish to hear my lecture, come to this temple at seven o'clock tonight." That is how he gathered the people. That is how he went on foot from the top to the bottom of Japan. On one of these crusades he met my teacher, Dr. Chujiro Hayashi, who later became the first disciple of Dr. Usui and the second Reiki Master.

As the time of Dr. Usui's death drew near, he passed the teachings and energy of Reiki onto Dr. Hayashi, a retired naval officer. Dr. Hayashi continued in Dr. Usui's traditions, traveling, teaching and dedicating his life to Reiki. Hawayo Takata met Dr. Hayashi, and through her perseverance and training with him, became a Reiki Master in 1938. Hawayo Takata brought Reiki into Hawaii, then into the United States in the 1970s. At the time of her death in 1980, there were approximately twenty-one Reiki Masters in the world.

Hawayo Takata's granddaughter, Phyllis Lei Furumoto, is the current Grand Master of

Reiki. There are now well over six hundred Reiki Masters who have received the required sacred initiations and undergone the long training necessary to earn a coveted membership in the Reiki Alliance (the professional association of Reiki Masters).

Reiki Masters dedicate themselves to living, being, and perpetuating the Universal Life Force. It is their honor and duty to assist with the harmony and balance of the universe, and to provide others with a means of balancing their body, mind and spirit. With almost six billion beings on this planet, there is a vital need for more Reiki Masters who can serve mankind and the universe in this wonderful way.

Five Spiritual Principles of REIKI

Just for Today I shall not Worry

Just for Today I shall do my work Honestly

Just for today I will not Anger

Just for Today I shall Respect and be
Kind to all Beings

Just for Today I will Accept my Many
Blessings

Acknowledge your Light
at all times and in all ways,
putting every thought
and action into the Light.

II

What is REIKI?

This is the Japanese character "Rei." "Rei" means spirit, air, essence of creation.

This is the Japanese character "Ki." "Ki" means power, or energy.

Reiki translates into Universal Life Force. "Rei" is the essence of the source of life. "Ki" is the energy or power that brings it into form.

Reiki is gentle but powerful, simple but effective. By simply placing one's hands on oneself or another, the Reiki energy flows, creating harmony and restoring the body, mind and spirit to its perfect, innate state of wellness. With the hands on the body, Reiki is on. With the hands off the body, Reiki is off. With this pure God-force moving through us, we never tire. It is not our energy being used; it is the love and power of creation in our unlimited universe.

The Reiki I energy involves receiving four initiations (or energy transfers) to align the chakras or energy centers. One of the unique happenings is that the hands become sensitized to imbalances in the body. The hands may respond by getting hot or feeling tingly. As long as the area of imbalance desires the energy, the hands will respond accordingly. When the imbalance is gone or that area has reached a "fullness" of Reiki for that moment, the hands will cool and lift off the body.

The Reiki flows from the universe into the crown chakra, at the top of the head, through to the third eye chakra, the throat chakra, and the heart chakra, then out the arms and hands to the person receiving the energy. Reiki is unique in that it is one of the few healing forms that can be used on oneself as well as on someone else.

The Reiki II energy accentuates the Reiki I energy for faster and deeper results. It is also an absent healing technique that can go anywhere to any individual requesting and desiring the Reiki. This is done with permission from the person who will utilize the energy. In Reiki II, one learns some of the ancient Sanskrit symbols that Dr. Usui studied in the Buddhist Sutras and received in his meditation experience on Mount Kura Yama.

When people receive the Reiki initiations, they are helped to begin their journey to spiral into oneness with their original creation.

As the hands are tools of discovery, there is no knowledge needed of anatomy or physiology. Reiki has divine intelligence and will seek its own path in discovering and fulfilling the body's requirement for this loving, healing force. Virtually anyone can be initiated into Reiki and have this tool for life. Infants upon birth have received the energy as well as the elderly or those with disabilities. Everyone responds well to this balance and harmony.

Reiki is powerful and consciously transformational. People become increasingly aware of their ability to be the best that they can be. Reiki is a compassionate, gentle, sweet path; it allows people to grow and heal as fast or as slowly as their karma and soul path dictates.

Reiki is used by professionals in traditional healing fields, thereby adding a wider range of modalities for their clients.

Reiki aligns individuals with the core of who they are. Once they have this energy, there is no return to a mundane existence. Life is full, fun, happy and whole!

Allow the degree of well-being
that you experience
so you can allow the same in others.

III

Illustrations of Hand Placements

The hand placements that follow are the traditional patterns taught by Reiki Masters to their students. When one receives a complete Reiki session by a Reiki practitioner, these are the areas touched. Usually the hands are on each part a minimum of five to seven minutes – unless the body signals the hands to remain longer. A Reiki session can easily last an hour or more.

If the client has a specific imbalance, there may not be time to go over all the placements. Instead, go to the head for ten to twenty minutes to calm the individual. This gets in touch intuitively with the mental thought forms that created the physical imbalance.

Then go to the area of the body that the client requests.

The hands rest very lightly and gently on the body. There is no manipulation or movement of the hands. The body is generally fully clothed, as Reiki, being a love force, has no barriers.

Maintain a relaxed but proper posture. Align your body comfortably with the area being touched. Do not put your body into stress in order to relieve stress. The comfort of the client who is receiving the energy is foremost at all times.

When the head, the front torso and the back torso have received Reiki, a complete session has been given. The legs and arms are not touched unless there is a specific imbalance.

FIGURE 1

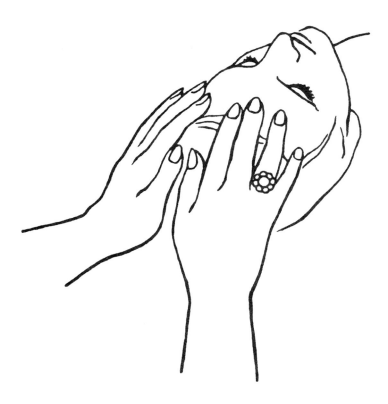

These positions are done with
the practitioner at the head of the individual

FIGURE 2

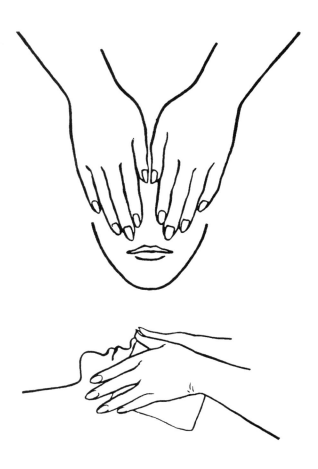

FIGURE 3

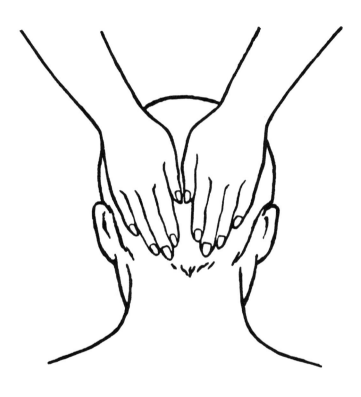

The individual is lying on his stomach

FIGURE 4

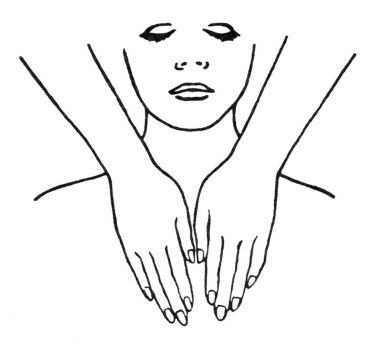

Figures 4, and 5, the individual is lying on her back

FIGURE 5

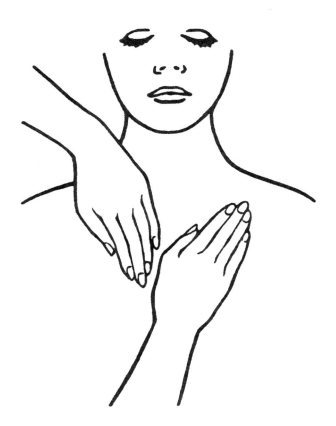

These positions are done with
the practitioner at the side of the individual

FIGURE 6

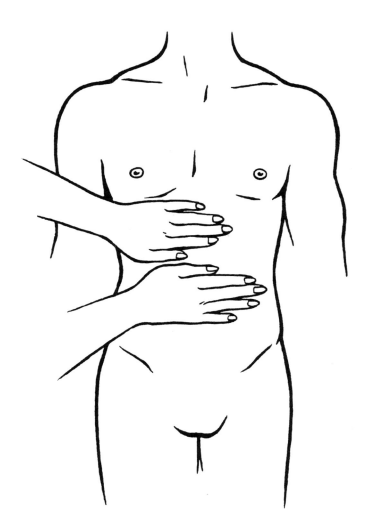

FIGURE 7

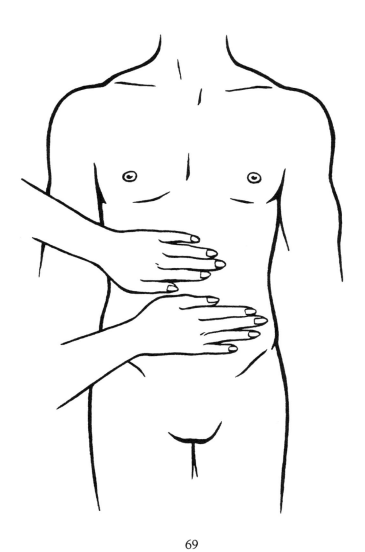

FIGURE 8

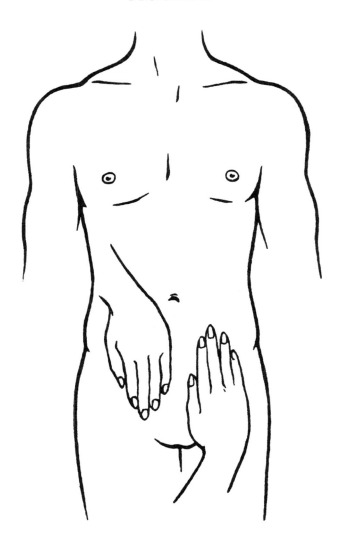

FIGURE 9

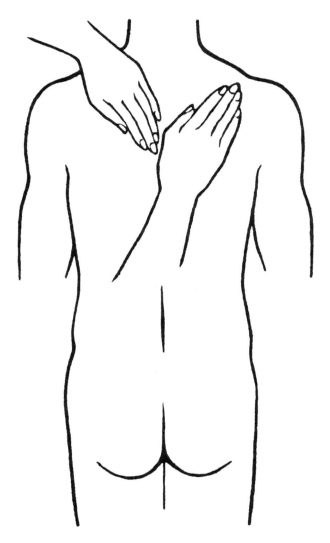

FIGURE 10

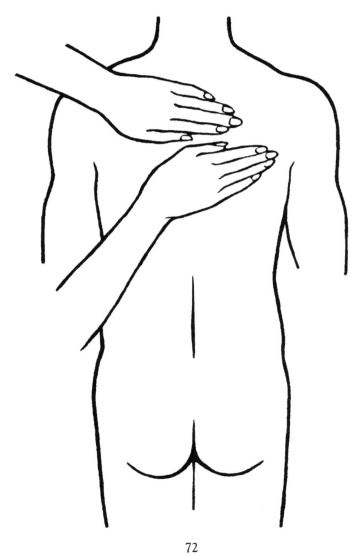

FIGURE 11

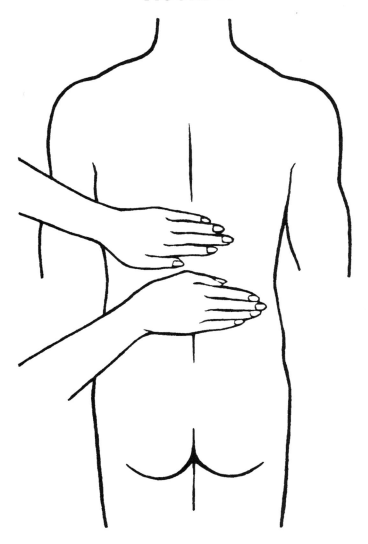

FIGURE 12

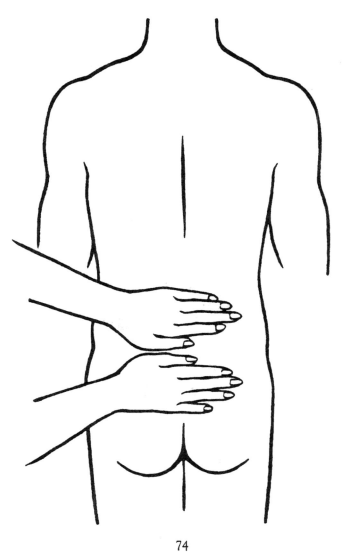

FIGURE 13

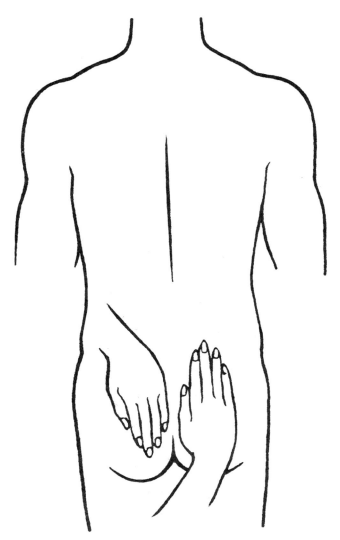

FIGURE 14

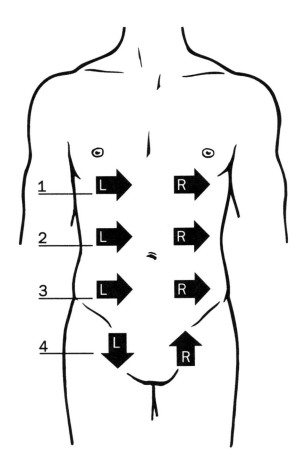

Treating Others – Body Front

FIGURE 15

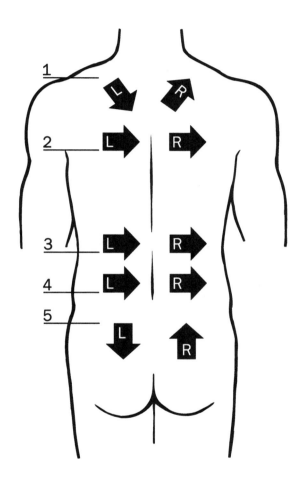

Treating Others – Back of Body

FIGURE 16

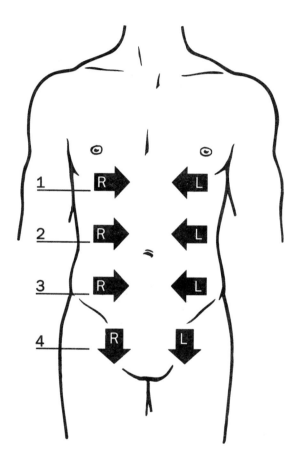

Self Treatment – Body Front

FIGURE 17

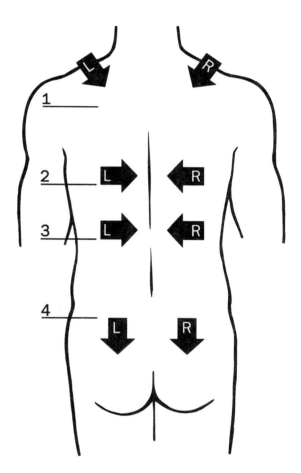

Self Treatment – Body Back

Success is doing everything
you know to do to make it happen.

IV

The REIKI Practitioner's Tools

Reiki practitioner's hands are their primary tools. It is also important to have a calm, restful atmosphere, such as meditative music on low volume, soft lights, and fresh flowers. Remember to unplug the telephone! Have set appointment times to monitor your energy and to set boundaries for your clients.

Have a table, such as a massage table, on which your client can be fully comfortable. You might add soft sheepskins for more comfort. Another thoughtful touch is to have various sizes of pillows to tuck under knees, shoulders, necks and ankles.

You may use candles and incense to keep the energy clear in the room. Many practitioners use crystals programmed to absorb and clear the energy. Invoking protection angels, such as St. Germain and St. Michael also helps keep the energy clear.

Be professional, well dressed, and organized at all times. Whether your client is someone you do not know, a personal friend or family member, always remember that they are trusting you with their body, mind and soul.

Have an attitude of listening, and when the client is on the table allow talking if he or she chooses. When questions are asked, answer the question – and only the question. Your client will hear the answer to that question, and may not be interested in everything you know.

Know that each person's soul chooses certain lessons to work through on this plane of existence. We all have our karma, and Reiki allows us to move through it in a subtle, gentle way. We give the same amount of Reiki to someone with a headache as we do to someone with a life-threatening illness. The one receiving the energy determines how little or how much Reiki is received. As practitioners, we need to put ourselves into a non-judgmental mind set. This allows all to be as well as their life path chooses.

Remember to have an exchange of energy so the value of Reiki is appreciated. In our Western culture it is the norm to be paid for our time. Reiki is a time-honored and legitimate healing technique. You paid to take the classes; it is important that you be paid for your time and energy. When someone has no money, ask if there is something of value he or she can barter with. Reiki is a great gift. When it is given away without an even exchange, an imbalance is created and the energy is not clear. Dr. Usui paid our dues for us in the beggar slums of Kyoto!

You cannot imagine or
make up anything
that you have not
experienced at some time.

V

Case Histories

Many Reiki practitioners are frequently asked if anyone has been "cured" with Reiki. The answer is that Reiki is an energy which brings the body, mind and spirit into balance and harmony. Even in traditional medicine, it is difficult to use the word "cure" or to guarantee any kind of absolute result. In Reiki we use the word "heal," which means to bring into wholeness on all levels.

As we work out our life choices, which often include physical imbalances, we are given the opportunity to understand ourselves better. Sometimes we can have great understanding with a stomach ache and resolve situations that caused that stomach ache. And if we don't learn from that simple imbalance, then sometimes a more serious situation, such as stomach ulcers, may slow us down in order for us to take the time to think about our lives.

Many people have been radically changed on many levels with applied Reiki, the Reiki lessons or both. Not only the ones directly experiencing the energy, but those around them can also be positively affected. Here are some experiences of Reiki healing.

A woman with metastasized bone cancer came to me for Reiki treatments. She had experienced sixteen surgeries in five years. On her first appointment she showed her most recent X-rays to me. I took these X-rays to several doctors in my building and asked them for their opinion. They told me not to bother giving her treatments, that her time was very short, and that I should not get involved in what was so obviously a lost cause. I replied that she had told me Reiki was her last resort, and that I could not turn her away.

This client committed to twenty-one consecutive days of Reiki treatments. There was no change, my hands never cooled off on any area of her body. The treatments were bringing her peace, calmness and less pain. However, because her doctors were telling her that her time was short, she and her husband wanted to take a vacation, which would have meant stopping the Reiki sessions. I told them I would rather that the Reiki be continued, that I had a "feeling" that more sessions would be helpful – but that it was their decision.

After discussing it at length, they decided

to sign up for a second series of twenty-one consecutive treatments. For the first eleven days, nothing different happened. Then, during the twelfth session, I looked down where my hands were on her body – but they had disappeared into her! I heard a sweet voice saying that she was healed. My client opened her eyes and said, "Something feels different."

I told her that my hands had reacted "differently" and perhaps she should go to her doctor and get some blood work and a bone scan. She did as I suggested, and her doctor reported that there was no cancer at all, anywhere in her body! I asked if she and her husband would come to my Reiki class the next weekend and not mention to anyone that she had been ill.

In the class, I introduced my client and

asked the students to do Reiki on her. I asked those present to demonstrate to me where the imbalances were in her body. While my client way lying on the table, the students were serious, their hands all searching for a place where the Reiki would activate to indicate the place of illness – but they found no such place. She was completely healed. My students asked me why I would bring someone into the class who was completely well. Then the client, her husband and I happily shared her remarkable healing experience.

This took place over ten years ago and this client is still as radiant as sunshine!

A preschool girl diagnosed with a brain tumor was given the Reiki I initiation and

Reiki energy during one session. Her parents also received the Reiki initiations at that time. The parents elected to follow the doctor's request to administer chemotherapy. The following morning that was done. Much later, that same day, the mother asked the doctor about side effects – when they might occur and what to expect. The doctor expressed surprise that the child was not already experiencing any side effects. In fact, she had been playing happily all day. The doctor said that this was most unusual – due both to the tumor and the amount of chemotherapy given.

The parents were allowed to take their daughter home, where they continued to practice Reiki on one another.

A nurse with pronated ankles called and asked if Reiki could help, stating that her turned-in ankles prohibited her from participating in many sports with her very active sons and husband. After one session with applied Reiki, she looked down and was amazed to see that her ankles were straight. Months later she called to say that they were "still straight."

This nurse, as well as many others in the medical profession, has used the Reiki energy to balance and harmonize her professional career as well as her family life.

A mother brought her fourteen month-old son in for the Reiki initiations. She said he slept restlessly and for very short periods of time. The next day she reported that he had slept through almost the whole night – for the very first time since he had been born.

Children who have had the Reiki initiations seem to have an increased compassion for other children. They become more kind and considerate. They love to offer Reiki to a friend who has a cut or bruise. In addition, they become more self-sufficient by giving themselves Reiki when they're hurting.

A teenage girl was thrown from a motorcycle, had a serious head injury and was in a coma. The family called and asked for the Reiki initiations to be done while she was in the intensive care unit. During the initiations, her eyes blinked and the machines started registering differently. A couple of weeks later, still in a coma, she was given therapy. Her parents were informed that, even if she came out of the coma, she would have to learn to talk and walk again. Weeks later she came out of the coma and the respiratory tube was removed. She very clearly spoke to the nurse, asking to see her father. The hospital personnel were very surprised, and asked her father what was going on. He tried to explain Reiki to them.

About five months after the accident the girl left the hospital. She was radiantly beautiful, strong enough to resume her ballet lessons, and dextrous enough to eat with chopsticks!

Kevin, a boy in his early teens, was brought into my office by his father. The boy had been diagnosed as having a malignant, inoperable brain tumor. His optic nerve was receiving pressure from this tumor, thereby impairing his vision. The family was given little hope of Kevin's recovery. After two Reiki applications and initiation into the Reiki energy, the boy's vision returned enough for him to go back to school and catch up on his homework.

Kevin continued the Reiki in my office, as well as practicing it on himself several times a day. At the same time he was receiving radiation treatments. After several months his doctors still wanted to continue with chemotherapy. The family had, by this time, all been initiated into Reiki and were bonded into the wellness of the whole group. The decision was left up to Kevin.

In the hospital, Kevin asked his doctors why he should have the chemotherapy, and if it would change the outcome. The doctors told him it would not change the outcome – but that was the only thing to do. Kevin responded that he thought there was something else that could help him. He chose not to receive the chemotherapy.

With Reiki, the tumor reduced slowly but surely. MRIs monitored the process. Kevin went back to school, and again became active in sports. A little more than a year later he was told that not a trace of the tumor was present!

Kevin Michael Appolito, age 16½, went to his "Field of Dreams" on August 20, 1990. Reiki gave Kevin three and one-half extra years of quality life in which he pursued all sports, particularly baseball. Kevin's last wish was to establish a foundation called "Field of Dreams" for underprivileged children to attend sports camps.

Other ways REIKI can be used ...

A psychologist working with abused children took the Reiki classes in order to administer a more loving and intuitive touch.

A learning disability school director took the Reiki classes to bring balance and harmony to herself and to her classes.

A gentleman, who loves to dance, comes regularly for Reiki on his feet so he can "keep on dancin'!"

Plastic surgeons are surprised how fast their patients heal with less swelling and bruising than usual.

In a third world country, the telephone lines were down. A lady needed to make an urgent call, but the operators told her to come back the next day. She put her hands on the telephone. Within five minutes the telephone lines opened and she was able to make her call!

The stories of Reiki are infinite and beautiful. Many have used Reiki to move themselves out of catastrophic situations. Many more use it as a daily practice, for a calming and more harmonious approach to life.

Reiki can be a turning inward, a gentle way to give love to oneself as well as to others. We are created in love. We can perpetuate that creation by acknowledging it in a more focused way with Reiki.

Love is the answer and Reiki is love.

May the 'Touch' be yours –
REIKI Master Judy-Carol Stewart

*Act on your guidance
and trust your information.*

VI

Letters from Health Care Professionals

"The addition of Reiki to a health practitioner's armamentarium should be required. Anyone who lays hands on a patient with the intention of diagnosing, examining, or healing should be trained in Reiki. The extra benefit this positive energy brings could touch the patient many times a day if every nurse, respiratory therapist, physical therapist, lab technician, physician's assistant or physician had taken a course in Reiki.

"Practically speaking, Reiki can do no harm – i.e. it's non-invasive and has no side-effects. From a scientific standpoint, it's still in the unproven stage. There have been no double-blinded, prospective studies to demonstrate its efficacy; however, every one of us has practiced anecdotal medicine at one time or another because it works. The explanations of mechanisms come later but don't change the results. From a healing viewpoint, Reiki's potential has no limits. Although it is still in the anecdotal stage, there have been some miraculous recorded healings.

"As an anesthesiologist, Reiki has become an integral part of my practice. I touch people every day, taking them through an event that's quite removed from their daily lives. I believe my Reiki instruction has helped me to communicate better at the non-verbal level. I can't claim to have lower malpractice insurance premiums than those who haven't taken Reiki, but I do feel my patients are significantly calmer and more relaxed since my Reiki initiations. This is no small benefit to their anesthetic management, and it's not one that can be included with their premedication.

"As a healing technique that's new to Western medicine, Reiki is a powerful but gentle addition to our traditional training. The only prerequisite is a pure heart and a desire to serve."

K.J. Kramer, M.D.
Reiki II

"In Western health care, traditionally the emphasis has been on the body primarily and the mind secondarily. The role of the spirit has more often than not been largely downplayed or ignored outright. The predominant focus has been on treating the pathological consequences of disease. The scientific method based on observation, that is what is perceived through the senses, is venerated.

"Intuition, or that which is discerned, rather than observed, is relegated to the realm of anecdote. A newer, welcome focus is on prevention of disease and overall wellness. Still, however, there is an under emphasis on the spiritual component, and hence the approach remains less then optimally integrated. An example is the treatment of addictive disease which has been difficult to treat. Only when body, mind and spirit are treated in an integrated manner does success appear with any consistency in these devastating disorders.

"The method of Reiki uses ageless principles and power, and concerns itself with alignment of body, mind and spirit. The focus here is on wellness, which is absence of disease, rather than on a reversal of pathological changes; such reversals are irrelevant in a state of wellness. Herein lies the distinction between healing and curing.

"Reiki is a healing art, an intuitive art, and relies on the healing power of love, the most potent force in the universe, or rather the force behind the very existence of the universe. It is a tool of profound significance and endless potential."

M. *Truett Bridges, Jr.*, M.D.
Reiki Master

A Letter from Kevin's Mother

"Reiki for me personally and professionally has meant awareness, acknowledgment and acceptance. As a healing power it was brought into my life as a result of our oldest son's illness from brain cancer. I previously had a sense that there was more to life and human potential than I had reached out for or could conceive of. It was within minutes of hearing of his diagnosis in the hospital that I attempted to make my first contact with Reiki Master Judy-Carol Stewart. Because of our positive experience with our son, I have acquired a tremendous understanding and respect for the healing power of Reiki.

"Our son's healing experience along with

my own personal experience with Reiki initiation has increased my awareness of life. There is now a greater sense of awareness for me of our individual connection and power with life. I now have an understanding for the energy of life beyond our physical existence. In working with my clients in the therapy setting, I am more conscious of how their own energy sets up the imbalances in their life. At the same time I have a greater degree of sensitivity for the energy and balances when they occur in the therapy setting.

"With this heightened awareness came acknowledgment. Acknowledgment of my own direct connection to life energy has allowed me to acknowledge my own power. I now feel I truly have a greater degree of acknowledgment for my clients' power.

Acknowledging their power has given me the ability to return the responsibility for their lives to them.

"Since my Reiki initiation I have sent a shift to a greater acceptance of my own emotion in my own personal life. This heightened sensitivity has enabled me to connect with and accept my clients' emotions, including their pain, to a greater degree. I feel that this shift away from my previously stronger analytical focus has allowed a balancing to occur in the therapy setting. This shift has allowed a true sense of acceptance for myself as a therapist and acceptance for my clients."

Dianne W. Appolito, M.S.W., C.S.W.
Individual and Family therapist
Reiki Professional Degree

Inform yourself
about the sounds
and colors of the universe.

VII

Learning More About REIKI

REIKI I

With this gentle but powerful, simple but effective energy, you can create harmony and balance within yourself and others. You will receive four initiations to align your chakras and awaken your hands so they are sensitive to imbalances. Reiki brings wholeness to the body – physically, the mind – mentally, and the soul – spiritually.

This compassionate and loving energy is an actual, ancient Tibetan healing technique that requires no belief system. There is nothing that Reiki will not affect. The word heard most often after a Reiki session is "peace."

Reiki I is for everyone, everything and every place on the planet and beyond.

Fee: U.S. $150

REIKI II

Reiki II is an advanced form of Reiki. It is used for distant or absent healing plus enhancing Reiki I energy for faster and deeper results. In Reiki II, you will learn some ancient sanskrit symbols that will enable you to bring someone's etheric body, mind and soul to you. You will then touch the etheric body with awareness of responses plus have the ability to communicate.

Reiki II allows you to tap into the memories of the cells to gain insight into the past, present and future. When this information is obtained, karmas can be removed and incredible positive growth occurs.

The symbols learned are held sacred and confidential. This information and power is only for serious and responsible individuals. Receive Reiki II initiations and claim this power to help heal yourself and the world!

<u>Fee: U.S. $500</u>

REIKI Professional Degree

My Dear Reiki Friends,
Congratulations on your courage to be!

The universe has its chosen few to lead the masses into consciousness. The responsibility is just that – to be responsible, to act, to lead and to carry the ones who cannot carry themselves. To carry the torch of life's light, and in so doing, to show others the way.

The world is changing rapidly in many ways so that only the ones who are prepared, who will accept the light role, will be left. Why do you think you will be left? To serve mankind. What will you need to serve mankind? Energy! Energy! Energy! How will you acquire that energy? Meditation, focus and initiation into higher levels of consciousness.

The Reiki Professional Degree is a wonderful way to achieve a quantum leap into higher consciousness. The Reiki Professional Degree is a statement to God, our planet, your family, and yourself that you are trained to fulfill your responsibilities to serve mankind.

In the Professional Degree you are given

the actual Reiki Master initiation, the highest amount of Reiki energy available to humanity. In addition, you will be taught one of the Reiki Master methods to activate this initiation energy so that you can enhance your life and augment your service to mankind by becoming the best you can be in your profession.

This initiation will change your life. Within a year you will be completely different – a new being – a spiritual warrior with the armor of right action.

Do not delay. Act on this immediately. It is available for you now because it is needed now.

Acknowledge your greatness! Do it now.

Fee: U.S. $10,000

More REIKI

I am frequently asked, "How does one become a Reiki Master?" One becomes a Reiki Master by being willing to totally surrender and focus on one thing – Reiki. Being a Reiki Master requires teaching Reiki and perpetuating the principles of Reiki to anyone, anywhere, any time. Reiki Masters dedicate and commit their lives to Reiki.

Being a Reiki Master is not a business or a profession that one does – it is something one becomes. A Reiki Master is Reiki, totally, completely, all the time.

When one feels his or her life choice is Reiki, that person studies with a Reiki Master who trains and initiates Reiki Masters. Each person goes through extensive and intensive lessons designed for that individual. Some of these lessons are basic – such as completing the Reiki I and II classes. Others are self-learning, such as how a Reiki Master candidate's astrological aspects will support him or her in this field. Everyone who trains comes from different backgrounds with different reasons for choosing Reiki as the sole path. In this way the world will be supplied with teachers who can convey information to all kinds of people everywhere.

Being a Reiki Master requires great sacrifice. Reiki Masters are willing to sacrifice everything for Reiki, which is love.

REIKI Master Third Degree

My Dear Future Reiki Masters,
Acknowledge your courage, your power, your greatness!

The final step in Reiki is Mastery. To be a Reiki Master is one of the highest callings available to humanity. Indeed, there are fewer Reiki Masters than any other profession on the world. It requires everything you are now and everything you are capable of becoming.

Reiki Masters are Reiki Teachers. By teaching Reiki we give humanity a way to be responsible for its own evolution – a way to bring balance and harmony to the world and everyone in it – a way to elevate the consciousness of mankind.

What is required of a Reiki Master? The desire to say "Yes" to God and the universe. To search for opportunities of serving. To focus on doing God's work in any way God asks for it to be done. Being a Reiki Master is putting your hand in God's with a vow to do God's work. Being a Reiki Master is surrendering and trusting the process of growth and change in God's creations. More than that, being a Reiki Master is allowing and assisting that change.

According to ancient scriptures, we are in the last of the four stages of time. The responsibility is greater than we can imagine. Some of us made a covenant with God that we would stay on the planet until all the work was done. Life is difficult but it can be made liveable, lovable and even sweet when mankind is taught Reiki as a way to heal itself.

Make a decision to take that final step – Reiki Mastery. Fill out your name. Reiki Master _____. How does it look? How does it feel? What does it make you think? Consider leaping into the void – which contains everything. Be the Teacher – the Reiki Master.

Acknowledge and claim your divinity! Do it now.

<u>Fee: U.S. $10,000</u>

OM

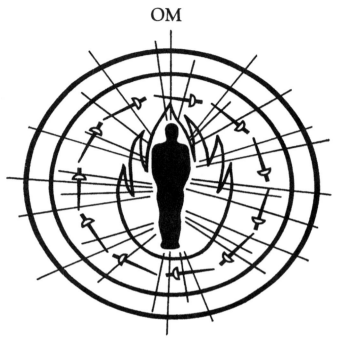

I am the UNIVERSE   I am
I am the SPHERE   I am
I am the LIGHT   I am
I am the FLAME   I am
I am the SWORD   I am
I am the REFLECTION   I am
I am the UNIVERSE   I am

REIKI Master Judy-Carol Stewart

Protection Method

We were created by God in order to serve God by serving His children, mankind. Our reason and purpose for being on this planet is to serve one another.

A way we can do that is to protect our own energy so we can use it to help ourselves and others. How many times, either in a crowd or after a conversation with someone, have you felt drained and tired? If our energy is not contained or protected, we are basically putting our mental, emotional and physical energy on a silver platter and serving it as hors d'oeuvres.

Observe the protection design. In the center you see a human form (you) surrounded by various spheres or balls. At the top is the word "Om" – the primordial sound of creation. It correlates with the first verse, "I am the Universe, I am." When this is spoken you are claiming your birthright, your existence. You are part of the whole, and the whole must have all of its parts.

The next line is, "I am the Sphere, I am." Look at the second from the outermost sphere. This one is your own design. In what do you feel protected? A sphere of gold? A sphere of rainbow colors? Create a safe sphere for yourself.

The verse, "I am the Light, I am," acknowledges that you are light, love and energy. Claim it by saying it.

"I am the Flame, I am," acknowledges the God of fire, Agni, who transmutes negative energy into positive energy by burning up whatever is harmful.

The ring of swords invokes St. Michael, the protection angel, by saying, "I am the Sword, I am." We are all spiritual warriors.

"I am the Reflection, I am," can acknowledge the rays of light shining from your being, or you can visually imagine a mirror reflecting out on the outermost sphere.

Close with gratitude, repeating, "I am the Universe, I am" – with the confidence that you are protected.

Do this every morning (for the day) and every evening (for the night) for the rest of your life. You may also repeat it anytime you feel the need.

Meditate...

Meditate...

Meditate...

Notes